How to Start Your Own Cleaning Business

How to Start Your Own Cleaning Business

*Low Start Up Cost,
Fast Growing and Profitable*

Sharron Jones

Copyright © 2016 by Sharron Jones.

Library of Congress Control Number: 2016905092
ISBN: Hardcover   978-1-5144-7973-5
           Softcover   978-1-5144-7972-8
           eBook   978-1-5144-7971-1

All rights reserved. No part of this book may be reproduced or transmitted in any form or by any means, electronic or mechanical, including photocopying, recording, or by any information storage and retrieval system, without permission in writing from the copyright owner.

Any people depicted in stock imagery provided by Thinkstock are models, and such images are being used for illustrative purposes only.
Certain stock imagery © Thinkstock.

Print information available on the last page.

Rev. date: 04/04/2016

To order additional copies of this book, contact:
Xlibris
1-888-795-4274
www.Xlibris.com
Orders@Xlibris.com
738854

CONTENTS

INTRODUCTION 1
BENEFITS OF A BUSINESS OWNER 9
STARTING UP YOUR OWN BUSINESS 15
MATERIALS 29
GETTING YOUR 1st CALL 33
THE WALK THROUGH 41
PROPOSAL/CONTRACT 43
CLEANING TIPS 49
BATHROOM 55
HERE ARE SOME TIPS
FOR SPRING/DEEP CLEANING 61
CONCLUSION 71
REFERENCES/RESOURCES 73
DEDICATION AND
ACKNOWLEDGEMENTS 83

INTRODUCTION

Are you struggling to make ends meet? Are you getting tired of living payday to payday? Perhaps, you are just looking for a change. Well I say, "Yes" it is time for a change. There are many reasons why people decide to go into business for themselves. I had no idea that I was going to start a profitable business. One day, my son came to me and said that he knew of someone who was considering hiring a cleaning company. He would have taken the job himself, but he couldn't fit it into his busy schedule.

He encouraged me to get a business license, permit, Federal Employer Identification Number (FEIN), and all the other pertinent credentials necessary for starting my own cleaning business.

I had just received my Federal Income Tax Refund and I had prior experience in the housekeeping field. So, this wasn't a bad idea. It would give me that second income that I was seeking.

I knew that I had my work cut out for me as far as finding out where and how to get this venture off the ground. I began to do a little research to find out the steps involved in pursuing my new career. I found out that it was important to write a business plan. I didn't have any experience in writing a business plan and I didn't know what information to include in this plan. I took a trip to the Library and found out that a business plan needed to include a mission statement, what type of service I would be providing and how I planned on making it a success. It needed to include who was going to be my targeted audience or clients? I needed to think of the area that I wanted to provide services in, and figure out the competition in that area. It was also important to know how I planned on marketing my business and getting myself known. I needed to include information about my business structure, was I going to do this alone or as a sole proprietor? Was I considering hiring a few employees and if so, how much will I pay them? I needed to think of any

and all things that would affect my business operations, such as permits, licensing, and regulatory issues, financing and any other pertinent information that will take effect on the business. It all needed to be written into a business plan. By doing this, it kept me on track. I could always go back to the business plan to see what I had accomplished and what still needed to be accomplished.

Every year new businesses are started, but many new businesses fail. This happens because new entrepreneurs don't have full understanding of the importance of the tax aspects or accounting aspects of their business.

This guide will give you a start. The Reference and Resource Page will list an accounting firm that will make this part of your business easy. They will file your quarterly taxes and prepare your payroll for you. A fee is charged

for this service. Feel free to seek your own accountant/payroll service.

In this Guide I will assist you in bringing your business plan together, and I have discussed the step-by-step process I used in starting up my own business. In the beginning you will get a few bumps and bruises along the way. Don't get discouraged. You could use this as a learning tool. I was fortunate because I took courses in Tax Preparation and also studied Paralegal. These skills made it easier for me to understand the formalities of becoming a business owner. I am writing this Guide because I would like to pass on to you my knowledge and experience in being a business owner of a cleaning company.

BENEFITS OF A BUSINESS OWNER

There are many benefits to owning your own business versus being an employee. You are your own boss and you are the decision maker. No more clocking in for your employer or having a set schedule. You work on your own terms, set your own schedule and you are free from answering to anyone. You call the shots because you are the decision maker. You will decide when and how the job gets done.

There are also many tax benefits when having your own business. Of course you must save your receipts. Most of these expenses can be deducted from sales and income (net profit), that is what you pay taxes on. You could deduct expenses like, supplies, equipment purchased or rented; postage, rents paid for business office or storage fees, utilities used, cell phone purchased and cell phone bill, etc. Your business vehicle could bring many deductions, such as parking fees and gas/mileage.

You could deduct insurance premiums for business insurance, gross wages paid to employees or wages paid to a subcontractor. This list could go on and on. Save your receipts to give to your accountant at the end of the year. Also, maintain a record of your expenses in a file. Utilizing Quicken or Quick Book computer software program is another way of keeping track of your expenses.

Becoming a business owner takes dedication, perseverance, and lots of hard work. The amount of effort that you put into this will eventually pay off. Being your own boss is a great responsibility. You will find yourself working harder than you've ever had to work before. To be successful, you must love what you do and do it well. Don't be greedy and learn to pace yourself. Allow your business to grow slowly. Start small and watch how you spend your money initially. Some businesses don't see profit until after their third year.

Some businesses don't make it because of lack of financial knowledge. That is why I am expressing to you my experiences in how

I am growing my business at a slow pace and watching it escalate into a profitable business. As your business grows, you will need an Accountant or a Payroll Service to perform your payroll and tax filings for you. Don't be afraid, it doesn't cost much and you will be surprised at the cost of hiring a Payroll Company. (See Reference Page for contact information). You may need an IT Computer Person to perform maintenance on your computer. Later, as it really gets off the ground, it is good for all businesses to have an Attorney. Most of all you need to have finances to start a business.

STARTING UP YOUR OWN BUSINESS

As stated in the introduction, you need to create a business plan. You are already on your way because you know what type of business you want to start. Now you need to decide a business name and structure: Sole Proprietorship, Corporation, Limited Liability Company, etc. Most importantly, you need to be legal. You will need license, permits, and registrations are required by all States. If you are running your business in another state besides D.C., please check your State's Licensing Board. This Guide will give you information for the District of Columbia. You must also meet the Federal Government requirement of owning a business. Call the Internal Revenue Service or go online to apply for your Federal Employer Identification Number. This Federal Tax Identification Number is assigned by the U.S. Internal Revenue Service for tax filing and other reporting purposes. It's misconceived that the first year in business is tax free. This is not true. If you make a profit at the end of

your first year in business, you will owe taxes. Hire an Accountant or a payroll agency to file your quarterly and end of the year taxes. (See the Reference and Resource Page for contact information).

However, there are fees to apply for your State License, Registrations and Permits. You must also register with your State Unemployment Office because you will have to pay State Unemployment taxes as well as the Federal. Check the State's Licensing Board to see if they offer one on one consultation in reference to licensing, and business tax information.

In the District of Columbia your registered business could have a trade name, which would be different from your own name. So you must file for this if your business name is different from your own. Be self explanatory in selecting a business name because your customer's first impression of your business is based on the name. You may want to think of a name that will coincide with the area that you want to service or where your office is

located. An example is "Metropolitan Cleaning Company". This would tell the customer that you want to service the Metropolitan area (D.C., Virginia, and Maryland) or the customer would know that you must be located in the Metropolitan area. You could also name your company a name that describes the type of service that you provide. An example would be "Quality Cleaning Crew". This would let your customers know that you are portraying that you provide quality services. Whatever you decide to name your business, make it easy to pronounce. Your trade name cannot be a duplicate of another business or cleaning company. One thing you should know is that if you decide to name your business a geographical name, it could limit your service to that area only.

These are the basic steps to setting up your business in any State. You will learn more by visiting your State Licensing Board. They may offer information to free programs, workshops, tax filing incentives and more for

new business owners. I know that it seems like a lot of red tape, but patience is a virtue. Remember that it will all pay off at the end.

You may want to contact an insurance company to get business insurance and bonding. First, check with the insurance company that you pay your homeowner's insurance or car insurance to. It is easier to deal with a company that you are already familiar with. Some clients will ask if you are bonded and insured. You may also need Worker's Compensation if you have employees. These things provide extra security in case something happens. Remember that at the end of the year you may use this as a tax write off. (See Reference and Resource Page for contact information).

Selling Yourself

What you put into your business, is what you get out of it. I can't say this more than enough. You must be energetic and creative

in getting your business out there. There are various ways of marketing your business. The cleaning business is a very fast growing, competitive business. Find out who your competitors are and why customers go to them. You may have to differentiate yourself from the competition. Be creative, have special offers, etc. You must find ways to get yourself known. Have some business flyers made, as well as business cards. This is a frugal way of advertising, because it doesn't cost much to have them made. (See the Reference and Resource Page for contact information). You may also choose to advertise in the local city paper for free. If you have the money, it is great to have someone build you a website. This shows a sense of seriousness and professionalism. (See Reference and Resource Page for contact information).

Check the yellow pages and call some of the local businesses listed. Ask to speak with the building managers or office managers. See if they have a cleaning service for their building or office. Send information to advertisements

that you may receive at home in your mail. Everyone at some point or another wants a professional to perform a cleaning service for them. It could be a one time job or contract. You may get a call to come in just to pick up unwanted items or just to do floor care. All money earned is good money. A small job, if done well, could lead up to a contract. Whatever you do, you must be prepared to do it. Perform the job well enough for the client to want you to come back. You will need a dependable vehicle to ride through your neighborhood and pass out flyers; post them where you legally can; give business cards to your friends, neighbors, local businesses, or ask if you could post a flyer in your neighborhood stores. The more you put out; the more you make people aware of your new business name. If you circulate 500 flyers, at least 1 person will contact you. Don't get discouraged, you are on your way. Later on, you may want to create a mailing list to send out brochures and flyers to prospective clients. You must get into networking with other business owners and professionals. You

should attend networking parties, webinars, and online discussion groups. You could learn a lot from networking and you may gain some business. (see Reference and Resources Page for contact information).

You will begin to receive all types of offers, invitations, and requests once you become licensed and registered. Get your company's name on a list with lots of merchants and businesses that belong to different organizations. Ask around. (see Reference and Resource Page for contact information). These businesses and organizations will help you get off the ground, grow and achieve your goals through educating or mentoring you. Most services are free of charge. Advertise your business on social networks, Facebook, Twitter, etc. Get a decal made for your vehicle. One of the easiest ways to get yourself off the ground is to get your family members to hire you first. Do the best job that you know how, so that they will ask you to come back or even refer you to a friend. Word of mouth is a great seller.

MATERIALS

You must purchase the essential products and equipment. You need to be ready to take on business when your first client responds. Some clients will supply their own products. If not, you must calculate the cost of the products into your quote. You will need the following for cleaning homes and/or commercial properties:

Dusters, Mops, Bucket with wringer, Broom, Dust Pan, Vacuum Cleaner, Vacuum Cleaner Bags, Paper Towels, Toilet Brush, Sponges, Brillo Pads, Gloves, Windex, Microfiber Cloths, an old toothbrush, Lysol Disinfectant, Ammonia, Magic Eraser, Multipurpose Cleaner, Stainless Steel Spray, Oven Cleaner, Degreaser, Endust or a furniture polish for multi-surface, Murphy Oil Soap, a heavy duty extension cord and couple of carrying cases to carry your products.

This is a good start up list. It will grow according to your clients needs. You will also

need office supplies and equipment such as a clip board, computer, modem, fax, scanner, copy machine, an office phone with voice mail. You will need paper products, such as; work order forms, invoices, letterhead, envelopes, and of course your daily essential office supplies. "See Reference/Resources Page for contact information". Remember to save all your receipts because this is a tax write off.

If you want to impress your clients, then you should invest in tee-shirts with pockets. You could have your business name printed on them for just a few extra dollars. This cost around $9.00 - $15.00 per shirt. The tee shirt could be worn with jeans or your choice of colored pants. It will make a nice uniform. Wear this with a pair of black work shoes or a tennis shoe. Whatever you decide, make sure that you are coordinating as a team. "See Reference/Resource Page for contact information."

GETTING YOUR 1st CALL

Getting your first client is like hitting the lottery or jackpot. Try to remain calm when you receive the call. Be a good listener and take notes of the request. Repeat the information back to the client to ensure that you have it correct. Ask for the spelling of the name and repeat the phone number and address given to you. Write down the basic details of the job and set up an appointment to do a walkthrough of the property. Never close a deal over the phone. You could give a basic quote, but explain that you would really need to see the property to be more accurate. Most jobs are based on the square footage of the property, multiplied by 15 cents per square foot. That is a formula used to come up with a basic fee. Once you see the property, then you may add on or deduct from that basic fee. It depends on whether you are satisfied with the amount that you come up with. An example would be a request to clean a two bedroom home or apartment or a request to clean an office the size of 1,020 square feet.

Multiply 1,020 square feet by 15. You would get a total of $153.00 as your basic fee to clean the property one time. Ask yourself, is it worth it for me to clean this for $153.00? You could add on to that fee if you are not happy with doing the job for that price. If you feel that $153.00 is too much for a one time clean, then subtract from the basic fee. You should also factor in the cost of products and special service fees. (See Reference\Resource Page for a list of some special services).

Now back to the $153.00, it doesn't seem like a lot of money. I want you to think about something for a minute, if you get an office this size to clean, it should only take about 40-60 minutes to do the job. Your monthly bill to clean this office one time per week would be around $600 per month. The bill would be higher for months with five weeks, instead of four. It is up to you if you want to kick in a free cleaning for that extra week or bill them for the extra week. Just imagine receiving three or more contracts this size. You could set it

up where you clean one office on Mondays, one on Wednesdays and the third on Fridays. Whatever works best for you!

Now, if I was to clean this same office five days per week (Mon-Fri). You would drop the daily cleaning price down to $30 - $50 per day (5 days divided by $153 = around $30 per clean per day) Factor in this: the office is less tedious because you are doing it daily, which will cut your time to clean in half. Also factor in that you are going more often, so you can charge more than the ($30 basic fee) $40 or even $50 per clean. This bill could range from $800 - $1,000 per month.

Again, this is just a formula I use to come up with basic fees. Just ask yourself, and consider all the overhead (products you supply, employee fees, extra services like changing of light bulbs) to determine what you want to charge. Now, just imagine if you had three contracts like this!

You will be more comfortable with setting prices as you learn the business. There are many formulas for creating quotes. This

is mine, just remember to factor in your overhead (your supplies, taxes, labor and of course your profit).

This is just the beginning. It is important to push yourself to market your new business as much as you can. Continue to work hard and you will see the results. In no time, you will reach three contracts. Set a goal that you want to achieve. Remember the sky is the limit.

THE WALK THROUGH

When you arrive at the walk through, be sure to take your work order form on a clip board. Look professional and be neat. No one will be expecting you to wear a suit, just be presentable. The first impression is the last impression. Be polite and introduce yourself, your company name along with whoever you take with you. Be a good listener and don't be afraid to ask questions. Some questions to ask are:

1. How did you hear about us?
2. Is this your first time using a cleaning company?
3. How soon are you looking to start?
4. Will you be supplying products?
5. Will I need to change the light bulbs?

These are general questions that give you a feel for the person and their needs. Allow the client to take you on the walk through of the property. When the walk through is complete, let the client know that you will email or fax them a quote. So don't forget to exchange business cards.

PROPOSAL/CONTRACT

Try to turn in your proposal within a few days. Once you turn in the proposal and it's accepted, you will need to write up a contract agreement. If you don't know how to write up a simple proposal or contract, then you may want to pay someone to do it for you. Dealing with the Government or some larger organizations will require more technical writing skills. When writing your proposal, make sure you include a cover letter addressing and thanking the person who took you on the walk through. Each area that needs service must be broken down; a detailed description of the services you plan to provide must be listed; and how often you plan on providing these services need to be written in the proposal. An example would be:

AREA: Bathroom

FREQUENCY 1 week

TASK: Clean and Sanitize sink, toilet, shower: wipe down mirror, polish all fixtures and sanitize door handles. Sweep and mop floors.

Continue to go down the list, listing each area that you are cleaning. At the end of the proposal, list your amount that you are bidding and have a signature line for you and the client. If the client accepts, you will need to write a contract.

It is important to have a contract agreement. The agreement is made between both parties and it gives the terms of the contract. It states that the client gives permission to you to do the job that you are hired to do. If the job isn't done in a satisfactory manner, then the client has a right to give you a time frame to improve yourself. If you don't improve within that time frame, then the client could cancel the contract. It should state when you will invoice the client and when the client is expected to make the payment. It should also state when the service begins and list your holidays. You could add any pertinent

information that you deem necessary. The contract needs to be dated and initialed or signed by both parties.

Once the proposal and contract is accepted and signed, then sit back, exhale and pat yourself on the back for landing your 1st contract. This process will repeat itself, just as long as you continue to work hard at marketing your business and perform the job efficiently and professionally.

CLEANING TIPS

The kitchen should be the first room that you clean. I say this because it takes the longest to clean and should be one of the cleanness rooms in the home. First wash all the dishes by putting them in the dishwasher. If the client doesn't have one, then wash them by hand. Dry them and put them away. If you use the dishwasher, then you could leave them in the dishwasher (unless the customer wants you to put them away). Clean all small appliances and wipe underneath everything (toasters, canisters, microwave, coffeemakers, etc.). If these small appliances have prints on them, take time and clean them off. The microwave should be cleaned inside and outside. When cleaning the stove, make sure that you lift up the burner plates to give the stove a good cleaning. If your client pays extra for cleaning the inside of the stove, you would need to apply oven cleaner and follow the directions on the can, unless it is a self-cleaning oven. You will not need

oven cleaner. Clean the top, front and sides of the stove by removing the knobs and getting out food, fingerprints and grease. If the stove has grease, then you may want to use a degreaser to clean with, along with a scouring pad. Be sure not to scratch the stove. If it is stainless steel appliances, then be sure to use stainless steel spray on all stainless steel appliances to give it a nice shine. Wipe down countertops, with the multi-surface spray. Wipe underneath the countertops as well as front and sides of the countertops. The cabinets could be cleaned with multi-surfaced spray as well. Be sure to remove all dirt from the cabinet knobs or handles. You would also need to wipe down thoroughly the refrigerator and dishwasher. Be sure to wipe down the sides and the top of these appliances. When cleaning the dishwasher, open the door and clean the inside. If the client wants the refrigerator cleaned inside, then you should charge extra. Clean sink, and polish all fixtures. You should do this next to last because you may

need to use the water while doing other chores in the kitchen. Be sure to getup all water spots. Lastly, you will sweep, mop or wax kitchen floors (if your customer has requested it).

BATHROOM

Clean the bathroom next because it too should always be one of the cleanness rooms in the home. Clean tub/shower stall, entire toilet inside and outside with multipurpose (disinfectant cleaner, one that has a nice mild aroma. Use a different rag to clean the toilet than you use to clean the rest of the bathroom. This is for sanitation purposes. Clean sink\countertops with multipurpose cleaner. Make sure that you remove all fingerprints from surfaces. Make sure that you shine\polish all chrome fixtures; shower heads, toilet handle, and faucets. Apply the multipurpose cleaner, then, dry it off with a paper towel to give it that extra shine. Spot clean the doors and inside of door frames because they tend to collect dust. If there are windows in the bathroom, wipe down the window sills. Use a separate rag and use Windex to clean the mirrors. Always sanitize the door knobs, sweep and mop the floors last. If your floor is small, you may want to clean it on your hands and knees. If this is a

spring cleaning, then you would wash down the baseboards.

General Living areas, such as living room, hallways, foyers, and bedrooms are cleaned in the same manner. First, start off with the dusting. Look in the corners for cobwebs and fingerprints on the walls. Dust away cobwebs and spot clean the doors. If your client wants you to spot clean walls, then remember to charge them more. Dust and wipe down all furnishings using your multi-surface spray. Wipe down the legs on furnishings and remember to wipe underneath tables and flat surfaced furniture. You will also need to dust any wall hangings, such as pictures. Once this is complete, then you may vacuum carpet or sweep and mop floors. Look like I have covered how to perform a general cleaning of a home.

If you are asked to perform a deep cleaning or a Spring cleaning, it is more detailed. You

would do all of the above, but you will need to spot clean all walls, clean all baseboards and wash the windows along with windows sill tracts and any sliding door tracts.

HERE ARE SOME TIPS FOR SPRING/DEEP CLEANING

WINDOWS

This is a very tedious task. They should be cleaned inside and outside, unless the client agrees to only cleaning the inside. Get a bucket of clean water and pour in one capful of ammonia. You may also use vinegar or just Windex. You will need a squeegee or maybe you could use newspaper. Newspaper is the old fashioned way of cleaning, and it will get the job done just as well. Wash the window down from top to bottom with the squeegee. Wipe the squeegee with a clean dry cloth to remove excess water. Repeat if needed. If you use the newspaper, then wash in a circular motion and then use a clean dry cloth to remove smears.

WINDOW SILL TRACTS/SLIDING DOOR TRACTS

These could be cleaned using the same solution as cleaning windows. Use a capful of ammonia mix in with your clean water. You will need a clean rag, a toothbrush to allow you to clean inside of tracts. Dip your rag inside of solution, squeeze it out and clean thoroughly. Use your toothbrush for hard to remove areas of the tracts.

BLINDS

You could dust blinds or use a multipurpose cleaner to clean dirt from blinds, if dirty.

BASEBOARDS

First, vacuum the baseboards to remove dust. Use your multipurpose cleaner to wash down the baseboards. Keep your rag clean. If marks and scuffs aren't easily removed from washing the baseboards down, then I suggest using a magic eraser to remove any and all hard to remove markings. When using a magic eraser, do not immerse it into a lot of water. You Just want to get it wet and then squeeze out excess water. Wipe gently, using an up\down movement. It works like magic! Once the magic eraser begins to tear, discard it and use a fresh one.

CEILING FIXTURES/CEILING VENTS

Use a long handled duster or use a clean rag and a stepstool or chair to clean fixtures, chandeliers, light fixtures, and ceiling vents. Chandeliers could be cleaned cautiously with Windex and a clean rag. There are online training tutorials to teach you different methods of cleaning. See Reference\Resources Page for contact information!

SPECIAL SERVICES

Cleaning inside refrigerators and stoves

Changing light bulbs

Cleaning garage\basements

Organizing

Ironing and folding clothes

Washing windows

Cooking

Running errands

Removing bulk trash

Lifting furniture

CONCLUSION

I hope that you found this Guide informative and resourceful in starting your new cleaning business. You should now know the basics of how to get started and have a good idea of what it takes to own your own cleaning business. So I have shared with you ways that contributed to my success. Take this information under your wings and fly with it!

Be creative, learn from your mistakes, and tap into as many resources as possible. Develop your own system to provide structure that will allow you to work consistently and efficiently. By doing this, you will create a company that will continuously grow.

Good Luck

REFERENCES/RESOURCES

Legalizing Your Business

Licenses and Permits

Department of Consumer and Regulatory Affairs
1100 4th Street, SW
Washington, DC 20024
www.dcra.gov
202 442-4400 or 202 442-4311

Federal Tax Registration (FEIN#)
Internal Revenue Service
Philadelphia, PA
ww.irs.gov
1800 829-1040 or 1054

DC Unemployment Tax Registration
202-698-7550

Bonding, Business Insurance, Worker's Comp
Erie Insurance Company
1610 K Street, NW
Washington, DC
202 628-1010

Corporate Payroll Services
301-610-9410

Flyers\Business Cards
Carol Stewart - 301-263-5751
cstewartbuttons@yahoo.com

www.vistaprint.com

Website Design
www.web.com
www.webhosting@yahoo.com

REFERENCES\RESOURCES

Business Lead Services
Home Advisor
www.homeadvisor.com
Red Beacon
www.redbeacon.com

Online Discussion Groups
www.linkedin.com
www.econnect.entrepreneur.com

Business Membership\Organizations
Small Business Administration
www.sba.gov

Score
www.score.com

National Federation of Independent Business
www.nfib.com

Payroll and Accounting Service
ADP Payroll Services
1-866-989-0196

Buying Cleaning Products\Equipment
www.uline.com
www.ebay.com
www.daycon.com

Office Products, Forms and Stationary
www.deluxe.com
www.officedepot.com
www.nebs.com
www.vistaprint.com

REFERENCE\RESOURCES

Uniforms Tee Shirts
www.aramark.com
1-800-785-2299

Starstruk Designs
240-839-1191

UBER PRINTS
www.uberprints.com
1-866-440-823 7

Business Listings and Advertising
www.yellowpages.com
www.salespider.com
www.merchantscircle.com
www.manta.com

Online Training Tutorials
www.housekeeping.about.com
www.ehow.com
www.youtube.com
www.cleangurulic.com

Proposal Writing Programs
www.cleanbid.net
www.biztree.com
www.cleanpeers.com

DEDICATION AND ACKNOWLEDGEMENTS

I would like to thank my late mother Mrs. Ada E. Jones for teaching me how to clean at a young age. She always instilled in her children that cleanliness is the next thing to Godliness. She always encouraged us to believe in ourselves and don't let others deter us from what we believe we could accomplish.

I would like to thank Christine Mills, Tammy Orebaugh, and Carol Stewart for critiquing my writing this Guide. I would like to thank my children Jonnel Herndon, Delonte and Benita Douglas, and my sister Santa Jones for being there for me, assisting me with passing out flyers and going on walk-through with me. I would also like to thank all of my employees who worked so hard, even when they knew that I couldn't afford to pay them much. A special thanks to Nacole Thrower and Leslie Bryant for making my flyers free of charge. Thanks to everyone who contributed in the smallest way to my success in this business.

www.ingramcontent.com/pod-product-compliance
Lightning Source LLC
Chambersburg PA
CBHW030916180526
45163CB00004B/1860